Aries

Also by Sally Kirkman

SALLY KIRKMAN

Aries

The Art of Living Well and Finding
Happiness According to Your Star Sign

HODDER

First published in Great Britain in 2018 by Hodder & Stoughton
An Hachette UK company

1

Copyright © Sally Kirkman 2018

A CIP catalogue record for this title is available from the British Library

Hardback ISBN 978 1 473 67667 1

Typeset in Celeste 11.5/17 pt by Palimpsest Book Production Limited,
Falkirk, Stirlingshire

Printed in the United States of America by LSC Communications

Hodder & Stoughton policy is to use papers that are natural,
renewable and recyclable products and made from wood grown in
sustainable forests. The logging and manufacturing processes are expected
to conform to the environmental regulations of the country of origin.

Hodder & Stoughton Ltd
Carmelite House
50 Victoria Embankment
London EC4Y 0DZ

www.hodder.co.uk

Contents

• • • • •

Introduction

• • • • •

Before computers, books or a shared language, people were fascinated by the movement of the stars and planets. They created stories and myths around them. We know that the Babylonians were one of the first people to record the zodiac, a few hundred years BC.

In ancient times, people experienced a close connection to the earth and the celestial realm. The adage 'As above, so below', that the movement of the planets and stars mirrored life on earth and human affairs, made perfect sense. Essentially, we were all one, and ancient people sought symbolic meaning in everything around them.

We are living in a very different world now, in

which scientific truth is paramount; yet many people are still seeking meaning. In a world where you have an abundance of choice, dominated by the social media culture that allows complete visibility into other people's lives, it can be hard to feel you belong or find purpose or think that the choices you are making are the right ones.

It's this calling for something more, the sense that there's a more profound truth beyond the objective and scientific, that leads people to astrology and similar disciplines that embrace a universal truth, an intuitive knowingness. Today astrology has a lot in common with spirituality, meditation, the Law of Attraction, a desire to know the cosmic order of things.

Astrology means 'language of the stars' and people today are rediscovering the usefulness of ancient wisdom. The universe is always talking to you; there are signs if you listen and the more you tune in, the more you feel guided by life. This is one of astrology's significant benefits, helping you to make sense of an increasingly unpredictable world.

Used well, astrology can guide you in making the best possible decisions in your life. It's an essential skill in your personal toolbox that enables you to navigate the ups and downs of life consciously and efficiently.

About this book

Astrology is an ancient art that helps you find meaning in the world. The majority of people to this day know their star sign, and horoscopes are growing increasingly popular in the media and online.

The modern reader understands that star signs are a helpful reference point in life. They not only offer valuable self-insight and guidance, but are indispensable when it comes to understanding other people, and living and working together in harmony.

This new and innovative pocket guide updates the ancient tradition of astrology to make it relevant and topical for today. It distils the wisdom of the star signs into an up-to-date format that's easy to read and digest, and fun and informative too. Covering a broad range of topics, it offers you insight and understanding into many different areas of your life. There are some unique sections you won't find anywhere else.

The style of the guide is geared towards you being able to maximise your strengths, so you can live well and use your knowledge of your star sign to your advantage. The more in tune you are with your zodiac sign, the higher your potential to lead a happy and fulfilled life.

The guide starts with a quick introduction to your star sign, in bullet point format. This not only reveals your star sign's ancient ruling principles, but brings astrology up-to-date, with your star sign mission, an appropriate quote for your sign and how best to describe your star sign in a tweet.

The first chapter is called 'Be True To Your Sign' and is one of the most important sections in the guide. It's a comprehensive look at all aspects of your star sign, helping define what makes you special, and explaining how the rich symbolism of your zodiac sign can reveal more about your character. For example, being born at a specific time of year and in a particular season is significant in itself.

This chapter focuses in depth on the individual attributes of your star sign in a way that's positive and uplifting. It offers a holistic view of your sign and is meant to inspire you. Within this section, you find out the reasons why your star sign traits and characteristics are unique to you.

There's a separate chapter towards the end of the guide that takes this star sign information to a new level. It's called 'Your Cosmic Gifts and Talents' and tells you what's individual about you from your star sign perspective. Most importantly, it highlights your skills and strengths, offering you clear examples of how to make the most of your natural birthright.

The guide touches on another important aspect of your star sign, in the chapters entitled 'Your Shadow Side' and 'Your Star Sign Secrets'. This reveals the potential weaknesses inherent within your star sign, and the tricks and habits you can fall into if you're not aware of them. The star sign secrets might surprise you.

There's guidance here about what you can focus on to minimise the shadow side of your star sign, and this is linked in particular to your opposite sign of the zodiac. You learn how opposing forces complement each other when you hold both ends of the spectrum, enabling them to work together.

Essentially, the art of astrology is about how to find balance in your life, to gain a sense of universal or cosmic order, so you feel in flow rather than pulled in different directions.

Other chapters in the guide provide revealing information about your love life and sex life. There are cosmic tips on how to work to your star sign strengths so you can attract and keep a fulfilling relationship, and lead a joyful sex life. There's also a guide to your love compatibility with all twelve star signs.

Career, money and prosperity is another essential section in the guide. These chapters offer you vital information on your purpose in life, and how to make the most of your potential out in the world. Your star sign skills and strengths are revealed, including what sort of job or profession suits you.

There are also helpful suggestions about what to avoid and what's not a good choice for you. There's a list of traditional careers associated with your star sign, to give you ideas about where you can excel in life if you require guidance on your future direction.

Also, there are chapters in the book on practical matters, like your health and well-being, your food and diet. These recommend the right kind of exercise for you, and how you can increase your vitality and nurture your mind, body and soul, depending on your star sign. There are individual yoga poses and tarot cards that have been carefully selected for you.

Further chapters reveal unique star sign information about your image and style. This includes whether there's a particular fashion that suits you, and how you can accentuate your look and make the most of your body.

There are even chapters that can help you decide where to go on holiday and who with, and how to decorate your home. There are some fun sections, including ideal gifts for your star sign, and ideas for films, books and music specific to your star sign.

Also, the guide has a comprehensive birthday section so you can find out which famous people share your birthday. You can discover who else is born under your star sign, people who may be your role models and whose careers or gifts you can aspire to. There are celebrity examples throughout the guide too, revealing more about the unique characteristics of your star sign.

At the end of the guide, there's a Question and Answer section, which explains the astrological terms used in the guide. It also offers answers to some general questions that often arise around astrology.

This theme is continued in a useful section entitled Additional Information. This describes the symmetry of astrology and shows you how different patterns connect the twelve star signs. If you're a beginner to astrology, this is your next stage, learning about the elements, the modes and the houses.

View this book as your blueprint, your guide to you and your future destiny. Enjoy discovering astrological revelations about you, and use this pocket guide to learn how to live well and find happiness according to your star sign.

A QUICK GUIDE TO ARIES

• • • • •

Aries Birthdays: 21 March to 19 April

Zodiac Symbol: The Ram

Ruling Planet: Mars

Mode/Element: Cardinal Fire

Colour: Red

Part of the Body: Head

Day of the Week: Tuesday

Top Traits: Energetic, Competitive, Independent

Your Star Sign Mission: to boldly venture into unknown territory, to set new trends

Best At: winning, going directly from A to B, grabbing adventure by the horns, thrill-seeking, fighting battles, being brave, the excitement of an adrenalin rush, blazing new trails

Weaknesses: impulsive, easily bored, argumentative, impatient, quick to anger, wants it 'now'

Key Phrase: I initiate

Aries Quote: 'After all, tomorrow is another day.' Scarlett O'Hara, *Gone With The Wind*

How to describe Aries in a Tweet: Mantra = me first; pushy, determined and competitive. Why walk when you can run? Wear red for passion, shout loud, take action fast

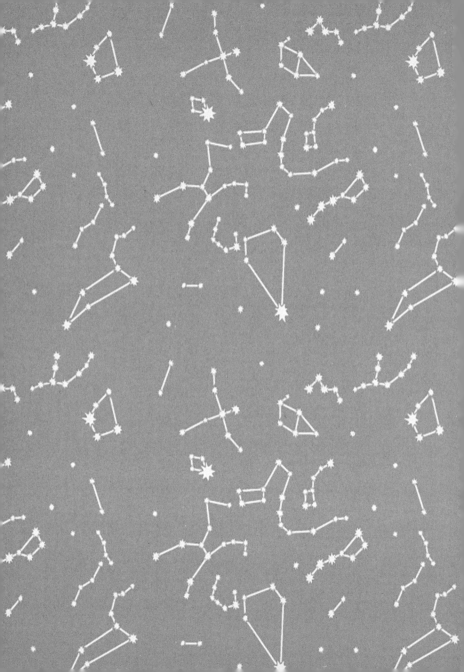

Be True To Your Sign

· · · · ·

The Sun's move into Aries is one of the most important planetary markers of the year and makes this the first sign of the zodiac. When the Sun is at 0 degrees Aries, it heralds the Spring Equinox and the beginning of the new astrological year. Winter turns into spring and your sign brings with it heat and intensity.

Your birthday month is a good time to go for it and be dynamic in your approach to life. What you start when the Sun is in Aries will line you up for success.

This is a time of new beginnings, reawakening after the winter with renewed energy. Therefore Aries is synonymous with being awake and all things new. It's symbolic of the young shoots that push through the earth at springtime ready to be born into life.

In fact, it doesn't matter what age you are; you are still capable of looking at the world through new eyes and there's a naivety and innocence about your sign that is beguiling. People being cynical makes you sad because you're at your best when you have a childlike wonder and appreciation of life.

You're often happiest seeking out new experiences and finding what else there is to discover, to do. You possess natural enthusiasm and energy and you're one of life's innovators, who adores the thrill of the new.

You are driven both by your desire to have fun and to be the first to try something, to set new trends. Spontaneity is your middle name. This becomes apparent when you consider what it means to be born under Aries, both a cardinal sign (leader/trailblazer) and a fire sign (motivator/

energiser). You like to be where the action's at and boredom acts as a catalyst to get you fired up and ready for action.

In fact, there's nothing slow about your sign. You're one of life's speed freaks, who enjoys the rush of excitement and keeping busy. The classic Aries is an adrenalin junkie who drives a fast car and enjoys competitive sports.

Also, Aries is linked to the first house in astrology, which is associated with the physical body; Aries is one of the most physical signs of the zodiac, as they are related to bold force and strength.

This is thanks to your ruling planet, Mars, the masculine planet, a symbol of courage and daring. You like to be on the go and taking care of your physical body throughout your lifetime is a top priority.

In mythology, Mars was god of war and the planet most linked to anger. Red is Mars' colour and symbolises fire, blood and passion; this is a heated and intense planetary ruler that represents the brave, fearless side of Aries. There's a fighting aspect to your sign too, which shows in your love of competition, your natural assertiveness and your willingness to confront injustice or bad behaviour head on.

Mars lends you a healthy ego and ego in Latin means 'I'. This isn't to say that you disregard what others are thinking or you aren't sensitive to other people's opinions, but your essence is egotistical in the real sense of the word. You're naturally self-sufficient.

This independent side to your character could turn your focus towards self-interest to ensure that you get what you want or need in life. Sometimes this is born out of self-preservation but other times it's because, if other people aren't quick enough, you simply take over rather than choose to delegate what needs doing.

Once you're aware of this tendency, you can use it to good effect by helping to motivate other people and only taking on those tasks that fit comfortably into your skill set or that you can achieve in record time.

It's a rare Aries who doesn't feel confident enough to stand up for themselves. Your sign is deemed the hero or heroine of the zodiac, and you're at your best when you're fighting a good cause or you're on a personal quest.

If you're typical of your sign, you exude bravado and you can be pushy and brash to get what you want. You tend to take a direct approach in all your relationships, which means that you quickly get to the crux of the matter and you're not afraid to be honest, sometimes blatantly so.

The Sun is 'exalted' in Aries, which means it's happy here. This is because the Sun symbolises the essential self and Aries is the sign of the ego, so the two fit hand in glove. Aries' key phrase is

'I initiate' and Aries at its purest is supremely self-assured. You can go far in life when you quite simply believe that you're the best.

What you do need to learn, especially in adulthood, is to complete what you start; this can be your Achilles heel. You love to leap into a new project, a new job, a new relationship but if you grow bored, it can be difficult for you to see things through.

Your habitual mode of behaviour is to act first and think second and there's often a high level of urgency to your activities. Think of your zodiac symbol the Ram; like the male sheep, you can charge through life at full tilt, raring to go. This potentially reckless or impulsive side of your nature means that at times you create more difficulty than is necessary.

If this willingness to live life on the edge and take the initiative is channelled effectively, then anything is possible. You live in the moment and as an Aries, you love to win and aim to be the best in all that you do. And more importantly than any other quality you possess, you will rarely give up without a fight.

Your Shadow Side

Did you know that your sign of Aries has a reputation for being the bad boy or bad girl of the zodiac? Your ruler Mars is god of war, after all.

Add to this the fact that you have a fearless, impetuous nature and your insane attraction to danger or getting into fights, and sometimes trouble is never far away. A recent survey suggested that there are more Aries in prison than any other sign, so rein in the angry, foolhardy side of your character and channel all that strength and passion into worthwhile activities.

You are one of the fire signs and Mars is the 'red' planet. Put the two together and you can be someone who's hot-headed and hot-blooded. You can literally 'see red' and you are renowned for your quick temper. Yours is the sign of fights, disputes, quarrels and controversy.

This has a lot to do with the fact that Aries is an honest and open sign. You have a natural bluntness and frankness that can rub people up the wrong way if they're not expecting it.

Use your anger constructively to persuade and rally others to action. Passion is infectious and this is where your heroic side comes into its own when you find your cause to champion. Your crusading zeal enables you to pioneer good deeds, defend the underdog and fight for your own and other people's rights. It's a much better mission in life than ending up in prison.

You are prone to impulsive behaviour too, acting before you think, and it's this side of your Aries personality that can lead you into trouble. Usually, your intention isn't to offend or upset the other person concerned, but you're naturally straight-forward and direct.

You can, however, learn from your opposite sign of Libra, the sign of relationships. Libra is associated with diplomacy and a typical Libra will always consider another person's feelings before acting, and they will even put their own feelings second to please someone else. For this charming air sign, there are two sides to every coin and they know how and when to compromise.

Your sign of Aries is independent by nature and you naturally put yourself first. If you can learn from the excellent negotiating skills of Libra and become less selfish, you might still get results without having to launch into an attack when things don't go your way.

Another point to mention about your shadow side is that you can sometimes lack sophistication, even going so far as to be rude, uncouth or vulgar. This goes hand in hand with a wicked sense of humour but it's not always to everyone's liking.

Your Star Sign Secrets

Shhh, don't tell anyone but your greatest fear is that you won't make anything of yourself. You want to be lauded for your achievements, to be recognised for your greatness, but some days you worry that you won't achieve anything special in life at all. This is Aries' star sign secret.

You have another secret too, which is related to how you want to be seen by other people. Because you come across as supremely confident, they don't know that behind the self-assured exterior, you're quaking in your boots. You know that being fearless is fantastic but sometimes you don't feel that way and you simply want to pull the duvet over your head and hide away.

Your Love Life

Knowing about your star sign is an absolute essential when it comes to love and relationships. Once you understand what drives you, nurtures you and keeps you happy in love, then you can be true to who you are rather than try to be someone you're not.

Plus, once you recognise your weak points when it comes to relationships (and everyone has them), you can learn to moderate them and focus instead on boosting your strengths to find happiness in love.

KEY CONCEPTS: sexual attraction, instant gratification, winning in love, healthily competitive, two independent people coming together

Cosmic Tip: think of your love life as a fire; keep it regularly stoked so it doesn't burn out.

Being in a relationship is very different from your usual independent approach to life and this is where you can learn a lot from your opposite sign of Libra. Libra is talented at compromise and knows how to balance different needs and wants when it comes to a relationship.

Contrary to popular opinion, you do enjoy being in a relationship and being in love. Yes, Aries is classically independent and self-oriented, but you're one of life's extroverts and you love the banter that a relationship brings. Being on your own for too long can grow tedious and it's via your connections with other people that your energy levels rise.

Your ideal partner is unlikely to be a romantic sweetheart type but instead, you'd be wise to seek out someone in life who's got as much get-up-and-go as you have. You need constant stimulation in your close relationships otherwise you can be quickly seduced by temptation.

If a lover is to keep you by their side, then seduction must play a vital role in your relationship. More than anything, it's important to keep the flame of love alive by spicing things up and ringing the changes, so love remains exciting and vibrant.

You do tend to wear your heart on your sleeve and you can be blatantly honest, which means that it's rare for secrets to creep into your love life. You might even be the type of Aries who thrives on a competitive love relationship and loves nothing more than a good argument to clear the air. You can even enjoy stirring up trouble for the sake of it.

Don't forget the dynamics of yin and yang in love either and, if you are a full-on 'masculine' Aries type, sometimes it's the person who knows how to calm you down and look after you who's the one for you.

One of the plusses of a lively love life is that even if you fall out for a short time, the joys of kissing and making up are more than worth it. This is an important way to keep your love life passionate and that's a must for you.

You do need your freedom however, and a love relationship won't last long if you're with a jealous partner or someone who's needy or overly sensitive. You can quickly lose respect for a partner if they show too much weakness in your eyes. Wimps are out; heroes are in.

In fact, your best relationship can be with a lover who's as active and independent as you are, someone who can take care of you and has their own life to lead. You're not going to find long-term satisfaction with a partner who just wants to stay at home and watch TV. In this way, when you come back together from your independent lifestyles, love feels fresh.

One note of warning when it comes to choosing a love partner. You do like to take risks and you enjoy living on the edge, flirting with danger. This means that sometimes you end up falling for the 'bad boy' or 'bad girl' stereotype, which can be fun for a short time but rarely leads to happiness in a long-term relationship.

Instead be with a partner who encourages you to be the best you can be. Then when you have your duvet days, you'll have another person in your life who's there to get you motivated. Your own personal cheerleader.

You do have to factor into a relationship the fact that you love to be the boss and sometimes you are happiest in a relationship where you can take charge and take on most of the responsibility. Whether you're male or female, you're often the partner who wears the trousers. You like to lead a relationship in the way that primarily works for you.

That's not to say that you always want to be the adult in a relationship. There is a side to your nature that is childlike and unworldly, and you are more vulnerable than other people might believe.

In love as in life, you enjoy having a playmate by your side and you will often do anything on a whim for the one you love. Sometimes it's the silly little things in a love relationship that mean the most to you.

If love does grow cold, you're unlikely to stick around for long unless you and your partner are both willing to work at love. Your basic philosophy is that no relationship is better than a bad relationship. If a partner is worth fighting for, it will trigger your inner strength and reveal a grit and determination on your part to work things out together. Once again this is when you'll be keen to play a leading role.

Patience isn't your forte though and if someone new comes along and unlocks the passion in your soul, you could be off like a shot. The same applies if you realise that your relationship has grown stale and is no longer giving you what you want. All relationships have a purpose and you more than most are likely to recognise when or if it's time to let love go.

Ultimately, you're an impulsive character, which can be your weakness but also your strength. You're upfront with your emotions and when you know you're in love, you don't hang around waiting for inspiration to strike. Whether it's a marriage proposal or moving in with a lover, your response will be direct and spontaneous.

Your Love Matches

Some star signs are a better love match for you than others. The classic combinations are the other two star signs from the same element as your sign, fire; in Aries' case, Leo and Sagittarius.

Yet, sometimes an 'easy' relationship doesn't stimulate you enough and you thrive in a relationship that adds an extra dimension to your life. This might include a clash of personalities that creates a fiery relationship, which is much more your thing.

It's also important to recognise that any star sign match can be a good match if you're willing to learn from each other and use astrological insight to understand more about what makes the other person tick. Here's a quick guide to your love matches with all twelve star signs:

Aries–Aries: Two Peas In A Pod

There is something of the duel about this pairing. Your ruling planet is Mars, god of war, and this is a feisty, impulsive, passionate combination. Together you are uber-competitive and you may love to initiate fights so you can kiss and make up. Boredom is your worst enemy.

Aries–Taurus: Next-Door Neighbours

This is a sexy combination of the first two signs of the zodiac. Aries is impulsive and bold, Taurus is sensual and persistent. You teach Taurus that taking risks is a blast and Taurus reins in your headstrong nature. Together you can have a lot of fun and achieve great things.

Aries–Gemini: Sexy Sextiles

There's always something to talk about or do in this relationship. You two have a strong rapport and get on like a house on fire; you can turn arguments into humorous anecdotes. Laugh-out-loud moments and witty repartee go hand in hand.

Aries–Cancer: Squaring Up To Each Other

This can be an instant attraction triggered by intense needs, but Cancer must remember that if desire tips over into neediness, you will be off like a shot. Cancer brings out the little boy or girl within you and your inner 'child' responds to Cancer's 'motherly' ways.

Aries–Leo: In Your Element

You thrive on action and Leo's the entertainment king or queen. Both of you can be dramatic and at times there may be a clash over who's Number One. As long as you make room for each other's egos within the relationship, this is a passionate union that blazes fast and furious.

Aries–Virgo: Soulmates

Aries and Virgo, the Ram meets the Virgin. Inherently different in personality: your nature is wild while Virgo is orderly. This combination can unleash hidden depths and passion. A lasting relationship, however, requires patience and less criticism on both sides.

Aries–Libra: Opposites Attract

You are naturally assertive and decisive, whereas Libra tends to avoid conflict and always considers the other person's point of view. Aries rules anger and Libra rules fairness and justice. Libra teaches you about compromise and you teach Libra how to get needs met.

Aries–Scorpio: Soulmates

Aries and Scorpio are both ruled by the planet Mars, god of war. This is an intense, passionate combination that can lead to a competitive relationship. Two strong individuals who are as determined and steely as each other.

Aries–Sagittarius: In Your Element

This is an adventurous and bold relationship, with both parties seeking out the next adrenalin rush. Staying put in one place isn't an option, although Sagittarius is more likely to enjoy the journey while you're eager to reach the destination.

Aries–Capricorn: Squaring Up To Each Other

This is a wicked combination, with each sign

bringing out the best (or worst) in each other. It's a 'male' and competitive pairing and both signs like to be on top. As long as you know who wears the trousers and that works for both of you, you can go far together.

Aries–Aquarius: Sexy Sextiles

Your passion for life shakes Aquarius out of their sometimes techno-dazed world. You two are the white knights of the zodiac and a mutual love of social, environmental or humanitarian concerns draws you close. Find your mission as a couple.

Aries–Pisces: Next-Door Neighbours

The Pisces–Aries couple can fall head over heels in love – and fast. Pisces' sentimentality may grate on you with your no-nonsense ways, and your impatience may drive sensitive Pisces a little batty. If you meet each other halfway, your love of and joy in life can be inspirational.

Your Sex Life

· · · · ·

It's worth mentioning the fact that one of the most famous lovers of all time, Casanova (2 April), was an Aries. You are a hot-blooded fire sign, after all. Add to this the fact that your ruling planet Mars is the symbol for the phallus and directly linked to sexuality, especially the libido, and when you're turned on, you're a hotbed of desire.

Aries is a passionate sign and whatever your sex, you usually love the thrill of the chase. In fact, it's a rare Aries who will wait for someone to come on to them. Your philosophy is that life's short and the quicker you act, the better. Therefore, if you can initiate a connection with someone new in your life, why wait?

You might be the type of Aries who loves the freedom of sexual relationships and doesn't want to be tied to one person. During the times in your life when you're free and single, you may decide to experiment and explore all that sex has to offer. If you're true to your sign, you have a high libido and you can enjoy the pleasure of sex without a romantic connection.

This free-and-easy approach to loving fits the theme of your ruler Mars. In Roman mythology, the god Mars was called Ares, and he never married but had many lovers. A casual attitude to love and sex can suit your nature, whether you're male or female.

In the 1970s, an Aries woman, Erica Jong (26 March) wrote a cult novel entitled *Fear of Flying*, in which she coined the phrase the 'zipless fuck'. This was primarily a sexual encounter between strangers free of ulterior motives and the book, with its focus on women's sexual desires, caused a sensation. The revolutionary ideas proved to be a revelation for women and men alike.

So experiment with your sexual nature to discover what pleasure means for you. This is where the free side of your character can truly come into its own.

Being an Aries, you're one of life's initiators and, just as you're likely to take the lead in attracting a lover, you're often happy to take the lead in bed as well. Whether you're an Aries man or an Aries woman, your favourite sex position is often on top where you can be in control and your approach to sex, in general, tends to be direct and to the point. Foreplay isn't necessarily an essential part of your lovemaking.

In fact, if anyone's going to enjoy a quickie and the chance of instant gratification when it comes to sex, it's Aries. Fast and furious is your approach to life so translate that into fast and furious lovemaking too. You have a lusty soul and a keen sense of excitement and adventure – in and out of bed – and your typical approach to sex is passionate, impetuous and fun.

Physical attraction tends to be a big turn-on for you too and you'll eye up a lover's body first before you find out more about their personality. This is especially true if you're into keeping fit and you're looking for an athletic partner in bed.

Sometimes, you need to be careful that you don't focus only on your own pleasure in the sexual act and to remember that there are two people involved. Otherwise, if you're too dominant in bed and you concentrate solely on your own sexual pleasure, a partner might quickly tire. Learn to give as well as take for an ultimately fulfilling and rewarding sexual experience.

ARIES ON A FIRST DATE

- You make a bold statement, in your choice of clothes or mode of transport

- You talk overexcitedly in a loud voice

- You constantly interrupt the other person

- You're argumentative and passionate in equal measure

- If you fancy them, you proposition them

Your Friends And Family

Find the right group of friends in your life at any given time and this is a sure-fire step in the direction of happiness. You need an outlet for the wild and extrovert side of your character and one quality that dominates the right kind of friendships for you is fun.

Find friends who you can have a laugh with and enjoy yourself with, friends who you can go on adventures with and make the most of life. It doesn't need to be the same set of friends either.

When it comes to making friends, you're not usually shy and you're rarely self-conscious, which means your true personality comes across. With you, people tend to know immediately what they're going to get.

On the whole, you fit happily into any social group, as long as other people aren't stuffy and pretentious. However, they might not always find your upfront character easy.

You tend to speak your mind, so some friendships can be short-lived. You're unlikely to waste too much time on a friendship that's unravelled and a typical Aries response is to issue an ultimatum, pick yourself up and move on.

Not everyone in life will warm to your strident nature and if a friendship or group is particularly important to you, there will be times when it's wise to rein in your forceful personality.

For a fulfilling life, veer towards groups where you can make a difference. Here you can tap into the crusading side of your character when you team up with other people of like minds with whom you share common goals and principles.

You also tend to slot easily into a leadership role as long as there aren't too many drawn-out and painfully slow committee meetings. If a decision needs to be made fast, you're the one.

One of your strengths when it comes to friendship is your ability to help others and you often can't help yourself if someone close to you is struggling. This is where your natural ability to take charge kicks in and you will move heaven and earth to find a solution to a friend's problem or issue.

You're quick to take sides too and to speak up if you feel that a friend has been poorly treated. If someone close finds it hard to show their anger, you'll be more than ready to step in to defend them and let rip.

In this respect, you're a loyal friend but with both friends and family, you're not always around consistently. You rarely make regular contact but instead are more likely to reach out when you feel like it. You'll be enthusiastic when you do so, even if you've not made contact for some time.

Family holds a special place in your heart and it's with your blood ties that your loyal nature is most likely to kick in. In fact, you will often do anything for the ones you love and this shows in your selfless nature. If your family are good to you, you go that extra mile for them.

Obviously, not all Aries family relationships are strong, especially if you've experienced a clash of personalities or your natural tendency to speak out has caused trouble between you. If so, you won't back down easily – unless you know you're in the wrong, and then you'll be the first to apologise. You still won't put up with a situation that proves uncomfortable day in, day out. In this respect, you're more likely to see one another less, no regrets.

As a parent or in your role as auntie, uncle or godparent, you're in your element. Children bring out your own fun-loving nature and they are a great excuse for you to be daft and silly. You rarely have a cloying or overly close relationship with a child; you know that your job is to teach a child how to be independent and to show them when breaking the rules in life can be a good thing.

You want to instil in any child values of honesty, inner strength and self-belief. If you can help them find their passion in life and experience joy at some point in every day, you've played your part and done your job.

Aries isn't thought of as a sign with excellent parenting skills and yet, if you decide to be a parent, you do it well. You have enough energy to be a single parent if you choose, or to adopt or nurture children who come into your life along the way.

Even though you'll happily take charge, the joy of your connection is that you meet one another at a child's level and that can be truly unique. It is important, however, to think hard about parenthood as it will bring extra responsibilities your way that might not fit in with your preferred free-wheeling lifestyle.

Your Health and Well-Being

KEY CONCEPTS: your body is your temple, bumps and bruises, fitness fanatic, fast food expert, spice is nice

Your sign of Aries rules the head and you can be headstrong when it comes to taking care of yourself. You often dash through life at top speed, which is why you are one of the most accident-prone signs of the zodiac.

Add to this the fact that you love adventure and your usual approach to life is to leap in head first and you can end up with more bumps and bruises than most. One of your life lessons is to learn to pace yourself.

Stress can take its toll too if you take on too much and a typical Aries is susceptible to headaches or migraines. This is why it's of vital importance for you to lead an active lifestyle and the more you put into your fitness routine, even on a daily level, the more energised you feel.

Running is a classic Aries activity, or going to the gym or an aerobics class; somewhere you can let off steam and shake off any troubles. Zumba was made for you, as it combines physical fitness with having fun.

Martial arts are a traditional Aries discipline, even named after your ruling planet, Mars. In fact, combat sports or competitive games, such as squash or judo, suit your Mars nature. If you know anger is an issue for you, this is the ideal arena in which to unleash any inner fury in a controlled way. Either that or a drumming class to release any pent-up frustration.

Don't forget the popular Boot Camp, which is ideal for Aries, especially if it's run by the military. You may, however, not take too well to being shouted at!

Not every Aries will love sport or be super-fit, but every one of you does need to find their own way to de-stress, even if you only play or run around outside. If you're overdoing it and burning the candle at both ends, you can quickly burn up too much energy; you have to be wary of burnout. Notice the 'fire'-related words.

As well as adopting a regular physical routine, it's a good idea for you to learn how to calm your mind and actively slow yourself down. A discipline like yoga or relaxation would be ideal to help you achieve a sense of inner peace.

As Aries rules the head, including the face, your ideal relaxation would be a facial or head massage. Even a trip to the hairdresser for a quick cut and blow-dry can perk up your spirits.

Positive thinking is another excellent attribute of your personal Aries toolbox, so ensure that you do whatever's necessary to get rid of negative thoughts and replace them with positive vibes. Hypnotherapy often works well for you, or you have may your own strategies to help you adopt a positive mindset.

One of the plusses of having a high rate of metabolism is the fact that a typical Aries rarely puts on weight. If you're leading too extreme a lifestyle and do gain extra pounds, you'll notice quickly. You're likely to do something about it straight away, and when it comes to diets or self-care, you want to attain immediate results.

In fact, you're more liable to opt for a strict or extreme diet so that you can achieve your fitness goals fast. You tend to have the determination to stay on track with your health goals and you can do it on your own, without a friend or fitness buddy by your side.

You rarely need extra encouragement when you're feeling strong, and you certainly don't want anyone else to hold you back. It's physical exercise that gives you the biggest buzz and makes you feel great inside and out.

Aries and Food

If you're a typical Aries with a hectic lifestyle, you want to eat your food fast and on the go. You probably already know, however, that this isn't great for your metabolism. The good news is that as a body-conscious sign, you're more likely than most to ensure that your food is healthy and nutritious, even when you're snacking.

At the same time, it's unlikely that you're someone who can be termed a gourmet when it comes to dining. That's not to say you don't enjoy your food, as long as the chef doesn't keep you waiting too long, but you have few airs and pretensions when it comes to what you eat.

The classic Aries likes their food straightforward and simple. You often think of proper food as being a full English breakfast or a classic beef-burger, and there's nothing wrong with that.

It is important though that your food has flavour; strong flavours come under the rulership of Mars, your planet. If you've ever wondered why your favourite food is a curry or chilli con carne, this is because Mars rules herbs, plants and spices such as garlic, nettle, onion, pepper, cayenne and paprika. Spicy food helps you sweat and suits your fire sign character.

Other Mars-ruled herbs and plants include basil, rhubarb and radish. Spiky plants such as brambles and nettles are also linked to your ruler.

It's important to keep your food clean and not indulge in too many rich or complex foods, or at least not mix them. Lots of dairy or red wine and cheese after dinner can leave you with a headache and the same often applies to a quick sugar fix.

Return to food that leaves you feeling good inside and out, although don't become holier-than-thou. One of the strengths of your Aries nature is that you can live it up a little (or a lot) and then return to a healthy diet.

The festival of Lent takes place when the Sun is in Aries and culminates at Easter, a time of fasting and feasting, another indicator that your diet can go through extreme phases. In general, you have a healthy immune system and your philosophy tends to be that life's too short to eat salad leaves day in, day out.

Do You Look Like An Aries?

You are one of the easiest signs to recognise by the way you walk. You have your head thrust forwards as you hurry, often in a rush to get from A to B. Your sign rules the head and some of you have a telltale frown between the eyes as if you've been marked by your zodiac symbol, the Ram's horns.

Red is your colour, and the archetypal Aries suits red hair or has a reddish tinge to their look, complete with sun-kissed freckles. The classic Aries has a sharp profile and angular features. Look for high cheekbones, a prominent nose and a direct, fixed gaze.

Your tendency to leap head first into life and your love of speed, combined with your fearless nature, can mean you end up getting into scrapes. You'll wear a burn or scar with pride, especially if there's a daring or hilarious tale attached to it.

Your Style and Image

Whether male or female, a classic cut suits you best and frilly, feminine clothes are out. You like any form of clothing that you can move freely in and that doesn't prohibit you doing anything fast.

If you're a sporty Aries, then you're more than happy wearing comfy fitness clothes. That doesn't mean that you want to hang out in baggy tracksuit bottoms; you're much more likely to choose a tight-fitting pair of leggings that show off your toned physique.

'Casual but smart' would be your ideal party wear although no doubt you have one or two 'killer' outfits in your wardrobe that are daring and tight. Ideally, however, you prefer clothes that you can just put on and go. You know it's the personality behind the clothes that makes the biggest statement.

You look great in a hat, as Aries rules the head, and you can get away with most hairstyles, although straight hair or a short dramatic cut tends to suit you best.

You're not afraid to shock others with your look and your natural inner strength means that you can get away wearing just about anything. This might be because you want to court controversy or you don't care that much about what other people think. Piercings and tattoos are common for Aries, and your desire to break the rules can show in your fashion sense too.

You have some cool role models in the fashion world, like Dame Vivienne Westwood (8 April), who brought modern punk fashion into the mainstream, and the artist Grayson Perry (24 March), who likes to dress as his alter ego 'Claire'. Both his style and his art are bright, colourful and extrovert, just like you.

For the ultimate outrageous dresser, however, you don't need to look further than Lady Gaga (28 March), who sensationally wore a 'dress' made entirely out of red meat. Next time you're heading out to a party wearing the same old outfit, stop and think whether it's time to let your inner extrovert out to play. Playing it safe isn't your style.

Finally, whenever you want to make a bold, confident statement, dress in red, your Aries colour.

Your Home

> **KEY CONCEPTS:** spring colours, wide open spaces, individual style, toys for the boys (and girls), modern art, a room for pleasure and a room to keep fit

Your Ideal Aries Home:

A modern loft apartment with plenty of space and windows to let in the light. Ideally, the apartment complex would have an indoor gym, a sauna and a garage to store your fast car or motorbike.

You were born at the onset of spring and bright spring colours make you feel happy, so you want your surroundings to look and feel fresh. Red is the colour most commonly associated with your sign but you also love deep pinks, oranges and other vibrant colours that bring a sense of light and fun to your living space.

It's important too that you have plenty of room to move around at home as you have boundless energy. If you're a typical Aries, you love to be outdoors and hate to feel constricted as you can easily become claustrophobic in a small space. Your ideal living area would be open-plan or rooms with high ceilings. Either that or have windows that you can throw open to let in the fresh air.

Aries individuals don't tend to be enthusiastic gardeners, so if where you live looks out onto a garden, it makes sense to have lots of attractive, colourful plants in pots; anything that's easy and saves you time. However, you probably wouldn't say no to living in the middle of nature, somewhere you can go running or walk into as soon as you're out the door.

At home, it's best not to have too much busyness or clutter or many precious but breakable objects. Instead, opt for solid pieces of furniture rather than anything unstable or too fragile. Your home needs to be functional and the furnishings practical, especially if you lead a busy, fast-paced lifestyle.

In fact, functionality is the key to your domestic bliss. You love to have everything to hand and the latest gadgets to make life easy. Do you love having 'toys' to play with at home, in line with your youthful spirit?

You're a child at heart, so gimmicks that keep you entertained are a top choice. Objects that make noise can appeal, e.g., wind chimes or an alarm clock that talks to you when it's time to wake up. Anything that's slightly mad or wacky suits your Aries nature.

The look of your home can be unique as you're not interested in being a copycat or keeping up with the Joneses. You like anything bold, such as patterns or prints that make a statement, and frivolity or frills are out. You want simple lines and clear-cut impressions. Small, fussy designs aren't for you. Instead, it's got to be big and dramatic.

Modern art that's colourful suits your personality and an artist who paints in bright colours will appeal. Vincent Van Gogh (30 March) was a Sun Aries and his artwork, featuring strong colours, would fit your style.

Some of you can be happy living alone and would love a bachelor pad. The function of your bedroom should primarily be pleasure, with somewhere you can hide your clutter as you dash in and get changed quickly.

If you have the money, a home gym would be high up on your wish list, allowing you to work up a sweat whenever you wanted. And a pool or outdoor lake to swim in, if your dream comes true.

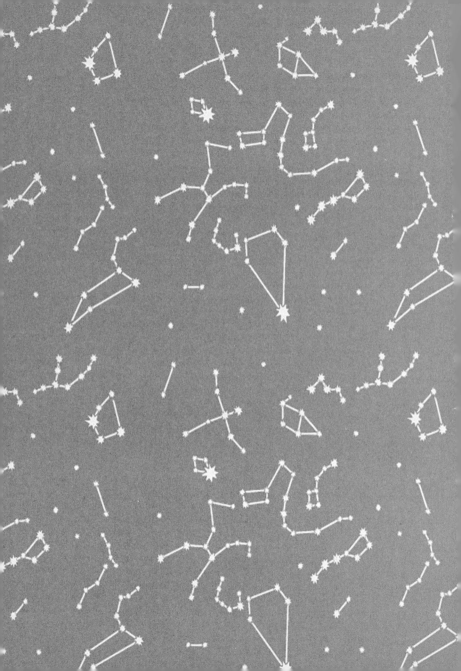

Your Star Sign Destinations

IDEAS FOR ARIES:

- *a trip to China to see the Terracotta Army*

- *visit Monaco for the Grand Prix*

- *a motorcycle or monster truck driving experience*

Did you know that many cities and countries are ruled by a particular star sign? This is based on when a country was founded, although sometimes, depending on their history, places have more than one star sign attributed to them.

This can help you decide where to go on holiday and it can also explain why there are certain places where you feel at home straight away.

You are one of the fire signs, who thrives on heat and warmth, so it's important that you get your share of sun. Head for the heat, especially during the winter months when you're more likely to need an extra burst of vitamin D.

Plus, unless you're running on empty and have to stop completely, you're liable to get bored on a beach holiday if it's too quiet. If you're having a good time with your mates, however, and partying at night, then a beach holiday can tick all the right boxes.

A solo holiday makes sense for you as you're so independent. You're often happy to join in with a new group of people and your extrovert nature lends itself well to finding your feet alongside individuals who share your hobbies or interests.

Adventure's your thing too and it can feel like a huge thrill to explore a country that's relatively undiscovered. You might, however, be just as happy seeking out an adrenalin rush on an activity weekend close to home.

Indeed, there needs to be an element of excitement in any trip away if you're to remember it for years to come. You might even be drawn towards danger in the places you visit or are fascinated by, e.g., a war zone.

Countries ruled by Aries include England, Germany, France, Poland, Syria

Cities ruled by Aries include Birmingham and Leicester in the UK; Florence, Naples and Verona in Italy; Marseilles in France; Krakow in Poland

Your Career and Vocation

The most important question any Aries must ask when it comes to career and vocation is 'What am I good at?'. If there's one quality that makes you stand out from the other eleven star signs, it's your desire to win, to excel in life, to be the first, to be champion.

So at some level, it doesn't matter what profession you choose to go into. Instead, what is important is that you're good at whatever you decide to do and that you have an above-average chance of being successful in your chosen career. Being the best at something is what ultimately makes you feel happy and proud.

Then when you're the best, you give it up and start all over again! That's not an unfair description of what happens for an Aries, because you are the ultimate self-starter and it's getting to the top of your profession or vocation that inspires you, not staying there. You love the thrill of the new.

In fact, many people born under the star sign of Aries have more than one career to their name, if not a few careers, by the time they retire. Retirement, too, is only an option if you're bored with what you're doing or you have a new goal to travel the world or fulfil a personal dream. Your sign is goal-oriented and without a purpose in life, you can quickly fade.

Keeping busy and being active are the hallmarks of your Aries nature, so a job outdoors ticks many boxes for you. Or a profession that's physical, one in which the body is emphasised and strength and stamina are essential components.

Many Sun Aries are drawn to a career that requires courage or daring. Mars is the god of war and even if you're not keen on a military career, you excel in any profession that's competitive. You might like the cut and thrust of a sales career or the trading floor, or any job that encourages you to put up a good fight.

Your fearless nature can be a tremendous asset in careers where you're on the front line, defending the weak or fighting for what you believe in. Aries is one of the white knights of the zodiac and championing a good cause or bringing about change in other people's lives is an excellent way to channel your aggressive yet altruistic nature.

Your quick reactions and the fact that you want

to see results fast can be a substantial benefit in some careers, e.g., working for the emergency services. What is also important to bear in mind is what *doesn't* work for you.

For example, you're going to be bored in jobs that are slow-paced or a career that doesn't fill you with joy or excitement. A back-room office job would be a real stretch for you unless you're working with a top set of people who keep you entertained day in, day out.

The other big no-no for you is being told what to do and most Aries know this in their heart of hearts. It's never easy for you to be in a situation where you get bossed around. You'd much rather be the one in charge, the one who gets to motivate and inspire others.

Ideally, you favour a business or career where you can work for yourself or be freelance. Variety is a key factor for you as your energy levels can dip quickly if you lose interest in whatever you're involved in.

If you're typical of your sign you have a big ego too, which needs an outlet in life, whether you head into showbiz or politics or become an expert in your own field. You do need to recognise, however, when your argumentative nature can get you into trouble, and know that some careers are better attuned than others to a strong personality.

Temper tantrums don't usually go down well in business but a cavalier approach to what you do in life can be an asset. In fact, if anyone's going to court controversy and get themselves noticed, your sign is up there.

In certain professions, it helps to have a thick skin and not worry too much about what other people think or take yourself too seriously. These intrinsic qualities of your sign of Aries can benefit you in life in many different roles.

Ideally, however, rein in your messiah complex if you have one and instead boldly go where other people fear to tread. You're a dynamic, go-getting fire sign who succeeds in life when you're allowed to do your own thing and do it well.

One of your strongest assets both in your career and in life is that you can be positive and chirpy even when things aren't working out. Your sign knows how to bounce back from failure and you're the first to seek out a positive response to any obstacle or setback.

If you are seeking inspiration for a new job, take a look at the list below, which reveals the traditional careers that come under the Aries archetype. Note that Mars rules knives in astrology, which will explain some of the Aries careers here.

TRADITIONAL ARIES CAREERS:

soldier

firefighter

rescue worker

paramedic

A&E nurse

stuntperson

racing car driver

athlete

martial arts expert

personal trainer

bouncer

butcher

barber/hairdresser

magistrate

campaigner

activist

lawyer

sports agent

project manager

motivational team leader

Your Money and Prosperity

KEY CONCEPTS: set up your own business, put important documents in your name, be entrepreneurial – take risks, make targeted goals

Money is rarely a goal on its own for an Aries unless you're fund-raising for a special event or seeking financial investment for a business idea. Instead, rather than having a fat bank account or acquiring possessions without a particular reason for doing so, you tend to be driven by glory and winning.

This has its plusses and minuses. First, you're unlikely to be someone who's going to save what you earn or who prefers a regular income to a more unpredictable salary. If you're a typical Aries, you find it annoying being frugal and would much rather lead a high-stakes lifestyle when it comes to money and prosperity.

In fact, it can be a thrill to know you can gamble on the next big venture paying off and the excitement attached to it when you boost your finances overnight. A money roller-coaster ride is often preferable to you to slogging away for a pittance.

You're not one of the star signs who usually worries overly about financial security either. Obviously, it's preferable if you're doing well and you can afford to buy what you want and choose how you spend your money. Any fear you experience in life, however, is less likely to be around money and not having enough than for some of the other star signs.

What does stand you in good stead about finances is your self-belief and your ability to remain positive even in the face of adversity. If anyone can sort out a deficit or tackle a debt issue, it's you. You have enough energy and the wherewithal to take charge of money matters when necessary.

In fact, sometimes you positively thrive when you find yourself in a money situation that's urgent or – God forbid – you end up in a desperate crisis. If you're a typical Aries, you'll roll up your sleeves and throw yourself 100% into getting back on track, and it can even bring an adrenalin rush. This is one of your best qualities: your relentless determination to ensure things work out for the best.

All fire signs, including Aries, do tend to have a remarkable optimism around money matters.

You're more interested in what money can offer you in life, e.g., adventure, freedom, than counting how much you have in the bank.

Your strategy tends to be high-risk and you're a confident entrepreneur at heart. Ultimately you're not afraid of failure, because you know that if you do make a mistake or a business or money-making idea doesn't work out, you can start over. You might even view this scenario as an exciting opportunity to try something new.

What does work well for you is to set yourself a financial target or goal and have a strong reason or purpose for doing so. This will help to keep you inspired. Ultimately you don't want to be held back in life by a lack of money but rather view making money as an enjoyable challenge.

It's not what money represents but what you can do with it that motivates you. You may be a stereotypical Aries who finds it a doddle fund-raising for others but not as easy to make money for yourself. If you have lots, that's a bonus but if you don't, you're unlikely to let it impair you enjoying your life.

Your Cosmic Gifts and Talents

Be A Pioneer

You're the first sign of the zodiac, and rightly so: so much about Aries is to do with being first. This makes you the pioneer, the one who's happy to lead the way, to be the first to try something new. You're the zodiac's self-starter, who's independent enough to boldly go where others fear to tread. Don't let fear or doubt hold you back in life – set new trends and start out on a new path. Be a pioneer.

Athletic Prowess

Not all Aries are going to be super-athletes but considering your sign is renowned for its speed, desire to win and strength and stamina, it's a natural outlet for your energy.

Check out the sports superstars in the birthday section below. They include a legend in motor racing, Ayrton Senna (21 March) and three of Britain's top gold medal-winning Olympians, Steve Redgrave (rower), and Chris Hoy and Jason Kenny (both cyclists). Weird cosmic fact: These three Olympians, plus athlete Mo Farah and the first man to run a mile in under four minutes, Roger Bannister, all share the same birthday – 23 March.

Rule-breaker

What are rules for, if not to be broken? If you're typical of your sign of Aries, you won't take kindly to following the herd or doing what you're told. You walk your own path in life and you're more likely to question what rules are for than follow them rigidly. This can be a good thing if used well.

If rules are stopping you or other people leading the life you choose, you want to know why. You might walk on the grass with the 'keep off' sign because you can or because you're defiant. There are many times in life when rules and laws need to be challenged. More often than not, you'll be at the front of the queue.

Cheerleader

A youthful spirit and a truckload of energy and enthusiasm are ideal qualities for the cheerleader. This is where you can have fun in life, motivating others to be the best they can be. You're a straight talker, who likes to keep things straightforward and uncomplicated, and you often inspire others with your direct approach to life. Whether you're cheerleading in the sports arena or cheering on your sales team, both cheering and leading are top Aries qualities.

Diva Behaviour

Fire signs make the best divas of the zodiac. There are a host of big stars born under Aries who are icons of the world of singing: Diana Ross (26 March), Mariah Carey (27 March), Celine Dion (30 March) from the girls and Elton John (25 March) from the boys.

Another name for diva is 'prima donna', which works beautifully for Aries, the 'first lady' of the zodiac. Divas demand the best and expect top treatment. Are you in touch with your inner diva? Are you prepared to be stroppy and temperamental to get what you want in life?

White Knight

Nothing angers you more than seeing other people mistreated or injustice in action. If you can do something to help someone's situation when they are in a weak position, you will. In fact, defending others or helping out is often where you find your real purpose in life. You're drawn towards charitable goals and your action-oriented, generous nature causes you to leap in. You're known as one of the white knights of the zodiac and it's a fitting title.

Honorary Redhead

You might be a typical Aries who has red hair and many Aries celebrities are either redheads or have a 'red' nickname or a name that alludes to the colour red, e.g., Reba 'Red' McEntire (28 March).

What's important however is that you recognise your own Aries characteristics that are associated with redheads: you're a fiery individual, passionate and strong; you get yourself noticed with your attitude, your swagger, your feisty nature. If you want more pizzazz and power in life and you're not a natural redhead, dye your hair red.

Films, Books, Music

• • • • •

Films: Any film starring screen legend Marlon Brando (3 April), e.g. *The Godfather* (1972), director Francis Ford Coppola (7 April) or *Brief Encounter* (1945) director David Lean (25 March)

Books: *The Silence of the Lambs* by Thomas Harris (11 April) or *I Know Why The Caged Bird Sings* by Maya Angelou (4 April)

Music: 'Happy' by Pharrell Williams (5 April) or 'Respect' by Aretha Franklin (25 March) or 'Rocket Man' by Elton John (25 March)

YOGA POSE:

warrior: for strength, focus and courage

TAROT CARD:

the Chariot

GIFTS TO BUY AN ARIES:

- a set of kitchen knives
- personalised jewellery; you love having your name immortalised
- any time-saving device
- a fast car driving experience
- calming bath oils
- rollerblades
- an exercise DVD
- a bunch of red roses
- red lingerie or mankini
- Star Gift - latest iPhone

Aries Celebrities Born On Your Birthday

MARCH

21 Ayrton Senna, Matthew Broderick, Rosie O'Donnell, Gary Oldman, Timothy Dalton, Ronaldinho, Rochelle Humes

22 William Shatner, James Patterson, Stephen Sondheim, Andrew Lloyd Webber, Reese Witherspoon

23 Joan Crawford, Akira Kurosawa, Steve Redgrave, Perez Hilton, Mo Farah, Chaka Khan, Roger Bannister, Chris Hoy, Jason Kenny, Gail Porter, Keri Russell, Princess Eugenie, Damon Albarn

24 Steve McQueen, Alan Sugar, Grayson Perry, Alyson Hannigan, Lara Flynn Boyle, Jessica Chastain, Tommy Hilfiger, Mary Berry

25 David Lean, Aretha Franklin, Elton John, Sarah Jessica Parker, Gloria Steinem, Marcia Cross, Big Sean, Casey Neistat

26 Leonard Nimoy, Diana Ross, Keira Knightley, Erica Jong, Steven Tyler, Kenny Chesney, Alan Arkin, Larry Page

27 Quentin Tarantino, Mariah Carey, Jessie J, Stacy 'Fergie' Ferguson, Maria Schneider

28 Michael Parkinson, Reba McEntire, Vince Vaughn, Lady Gaga, Zoella, Lacey Turner, Julia Stiles

29 Elle Macpherson, Eric Idle, Lucy Lawless, Vangelis

30 Vincent Van Gogh, Warren Beatty, Piers Morgan, Celine Dion, Eric Clapton, Norah Jones

31 Christopher Walken, Robbie Coltrane, Ewan McGregor, Angus Young

APRIL

1 Debbie Reynolds, Ali MacGraw, Gil Scott-Heron, Phillip Schofield, Chris Evans, Leona Lewis, Susan Boyle, Rachel Maddow

2 Casanova, Alec Guinness, Penelope Keith, Linford Christie, Marvin Gaye, Helen

Chamberlain, Michael Fassbender, John Thomson

3 Marlon Brando, Doris Day, Eddie Murphy, Alec Baldwin, Coleen Rooney, Rachel Bloom, Paris Jackson

4 Anthony Perkins, Graham Norton, Robert Downey Jr, David Blaine, Maya Angelou, Heath Ledger, Jane McDonald, Johnny Borrell

5 Gregory Peck, Spencer Tracy, Bette Davis, Jane Asher, Pharrell Williams

6 Max Clifford, Mylene Klass, Rory Bremner

7 David Frost, Ravi Shankar, James Garner, Billie Holiday, Francis Ford Coppola, Jackie Chan, Russell Crowe, Andrew Sachs, John Oates, Tim Peake

8 Betty Ford, Vivienne Westwood, Julian Lennon, Patricia Arquette, Robin Wright

9 Hugh Hefner, Kristen Stewart, Dennis Quaid, Marc Jacobs, Cynthia Nixon, Jenna Jameson, Rachel Stevens, Jesse McCartney

10 Omar Sharif, Max von Sydow, Gloria Hunniford, Steven Seagal, Mandy Moore, Lesley Garrett, Charlie Hunnam, Sophie Ellis-Bextor, Shay Mitchell

11 Thomas Harris, Jeremy Clarkson, Cerys Matthews, Joss Stone, Alessandra Ambrosio

12 David Letterman, Flavio Briatore, Claire Danes, Brian McFadden, David Cassidy, Shannen Doherty, Tom Clancy, Andy Garcia, Saoirse Ronan

13 Guy Fawkes, Thomas Jefferson, Samuel Beckett, Ron Perlman

14 Frank Serpico, Rod Steiger, Robert Carlyle, Adrien Brody, Sarah Michelle Gellar, Loretta Lynn, Abigail Breslin, Peter Capaldi

15 Leonardo Da Vinci, Henry James, Bessie Smith, Seth Rogen, Emma Thompson, Emma Watson, Samantha Fox

16 Charlie Chaplin, Spike Milligan, Jimmy Osmond, Peter Ustinov, Lynne Franks, Dusty Springfield, Ellen Barkin, Akon, Claire Foy

17 William Holden, J. P. Morgan, Sean Bean, Victoria Beckham, Jennifer Garner, Liz Phair, Rooney Mara

18 David Tennant, James Woods, Kourtney Kardashian, Conan O'Brien, America Ferrera, Rosie Huntington-Whiteley, Maria Bello, Tom Hughes

19 Dudley Moore, Tim Curry, Jayne Mansfield, Ruby Wax, Kelly Holmes, Kate Hudson, Sue Barker, Maria Sharapova, James Franco, Ashley Judd

20 (Miranda Kerr – born on the cusp, see Q&A)

Q&A Section

· · · · ·

Q. What is the difference between a Sun sign and a Star sign?

A. They are the same thing. The Sun spends one month in each of the twelve star signs every year, so if you were born on 1 January, you are a Sun Capricorn. In astronomy, the Sun is termed a star rather than a planet, which is why the two names are interchangeable. The term 'zodiac sign', too, means the same as Sun sign and Star sign and is another way of describing which one of the twelve star signs you are, e.g. Sun Capricorn.

Q. What does it mean if I'm born on the cusp?

A. Being born on the cusp means that you were born on a day when the Sun moves from one of the twelve zodiac signs into the next. However, the Sun doesn't change signs at the same time each year. Sometimes it can be a day earlier or a day later. In the celebrity birthday section of the book, names in brackets mean that this person's birthday falls into this category.

If you know your complete birth data, including the date, time and place you were born, you can find out definitively what Sun sign you are. You do this by either checking an ephemeris (a planetary table) or asking an astrologer. For example, if a baby were born on 20 January 2018, it would be Sun Capricorn if born before 03:09 GMT or Sun Aquarius if born after 03:09 GMT. A year earlier, the Sun left Capricorn a day earlier and entered Aquarius on 19 January 2017, at 21:24 GMT. Each year the time changes are slightly different.

Q. Has my sign of the zodiac changed since I was born?

A. Every now and again, the media talks about a new sign of the zodiac called Ophiuchus and about there now being thirteen signs. This means that you're unlikely to be the same Sun sign as you always thought you were.

This method is based on fixing the Sun's movement to the star constellations in the sky, and is called 'sidereal' astrology. It's used traditionally in India and other Asian countries.

The star constellations are merely namesakes for the twelve zodiac signs. In western astrology, the zodiac is divided into twelve equal parts that are in sync with the seasons. This method is called 'tropical' astrology. The star constellations and the zodiac signs aren't the same.

Astrology is based on a beautiful pattern of symmetry (see Additional Information) and it wouldn't be the same if a thirteenth sign were introduced into the pattern. So never fear, no one is going to have to say their star sign is Ophiuchus, a name nobody even knows how to pronounce!

Q. Is astrology still relevant to me if I was born in the southern hemisphere?

A. Yes, astrology is unquestionably relevant to you. Astrology's origins, however, were founded in the northern hemisphere, which is why the Spring Equinox coincides with the Sun's move into Aries, the first sign of the zodiac. In the southern hemisphere, the seasons are reversed. Babylonian, Egyptian and Greek and Roman astrology are the forebears of modern-day astrology, and all of these civilisations were located in the northern hemisphere.

• • • • •

Q. Should I read my Sun sign, Moon sign and Ascendant sign?

A. If you know your horoscope or you have drawn up an astrology wheel for the time of your birth, you will be aware that you are more than your Sun sign. The Sun is the most important star in the sky, however, because the other planets revolve around it, and your horoscope in the media is based on Sun signs. The Sun represents your essence, who you are striving to become throughout your lifetime.

The Sun, Moon and Ascendant together give you a broader impression of yourself as all three reveal further elements about your personality. If you know your Moon and Ascendant signs, you can read all three books to gain further insight into who you are. It's also a good idea to read the Sun sign book that relates to your partner, parents, children, best friends, even your boss for a better understanding of their characters too.

Q. Is astrology a mix of fate and free will?

A. Yes. Astrology is not causal, i.e. the planets don't cause things to happen in your life; instead, the two are interconnected, hence the saying 'As above, so below'. The symbolism of the planets' movements mirrors what's happening on earth and in your personal experience of life.

You can choose to sit back and let your life unfold, or you can decide the best course of action available to you. In this way, you are combining your fate and free will, and this is one of astrology's major purposes in life. A knowledge of astrology can help you live more authentically, and it offers you a fresh perspective on how best to make progress in your life.

Q. What does it mean if I don't identify with my Sun sign? Is there a reason for this?

A. The majority of people identify with their Sun sign, and it is thought that one route to fulfilment is to grow into your Sun sign. You do get the odd exception, however.

For example, a Pisces man was adamant that he wasn't at all romantic, mystical, creative or caring, all typical Pisces archetypes. It turned out he'd spent the whole of his adult life working in the oil industry and lived primarily on the sea. Neptune is one of Pisces' ruling planets and god of the sea and Pisces rules all liquids, including oil. There's the Pisces connection.

Q. What's the difference between astrology and astronomy?

A. Astrology means 'language of the stars', whereas astronomy means 'mapping of the stars'. Traditionally, they were considered one discipline, one form of study and they coexisted together for many hundreds of years. Since the dawn of the Scientific Age, however, they have split apart.

Astronomy is the scientific strand, calculating and logging the movement of the planets, whereas astrology is the interpretation of the movement of the stars. Astrology works on a symbolic and intuitive level to offer guidance and insight. It reunites you with a universal truth, a knowingness that can sometimes get lost in place of an objective, scientific truth. Both are of value.

Q. What is a cosmic marriage in astrology?

A. One of the classic indicators of a relation-ship that's a match made in heaven is the union of the Sun and Moon. When they fall close to each other in the same sign in the birth charts of you and your partner, this is called a cosmic marriage. In astrology, the Sun and Moon are the king and queen of the heavens; the Sun is a masculine energy, and the Moon a feminine energy. They represent the eternal cycle of day and night, yin and yang.

Q. What does the Saturn Return mean?

A. In traditional astrology, Saturn was the furthest planet from the Sun, representing boundaries and the end of the universe. Saturn is linked to karma and time, and represents authority, structure and responsibility. It takes Saturn twenty-nine to thirty years to make a complete cycle of the zodiac and return to the place where it was when you were born.

This is what people mean when they talk about their Saturn Return; it's the astrological coming of age. Turning thirty can be a soul-searching time, when you examine how far you've come in life and whether you're on the right track. It's a watershed moment, a reality check and a defining stage of adulthood. The decisions you make during your Saturn Return are crucial, whether they represent endings or new commitments. Either way, it's the start of an important stage in your life path.

Additional Information

•••••

The Symmetry of Astrology

There is a beautiful symmetry to the zodiac (see horoscope wheel). There are twelve zodiac signs, which can be divided into two sets of 'introvert' and 'extrovert' signs, four elements (fire, earth, air, water), three modes (cardinal, fixed, mutable) and six pairs of opposite signs.

One of the values of astrology is in bringing opposites together, showing how they complement each other and work together and, in so doing, restore unity. The horoscope wheel represents the cyclical nature of life.

Aries *(March 21–April 19)*
Taurus *(April 20–May 20)*
Gemini *(May 21–June 20)*
Cancer *(June 21–July 22)*
Leo *(July 23–August 22)*
Virgo *(August 23–September 22)*
Libra *(September 23–October 23)*
Scorpio *(October 24–November 22)*
Sagittarius *(November 23–December 21)*
Capricorn *(December 22–January 20)*
Aquarius *(January 21–February 18)*
Pisces *(February 19–March 20)*

ELEMENTS

There are four elements in astrology and three signs allocated to each. The elements are:

fire – Aries, Leo, Sagittarius
earth – Taurus, Virgo, Capricorn
air – Gemini, Libra, Aquarius
water – Cancer, Scorpio, Pisces

What each element represents:

Fire – fire blazes bright and fire types are inspirational, motivational, adventurous and love creativity and play

Earth – earth is grounding and solid, and earth rules money, security, practicality, the physical body and slow living

Air – air is intangible and vast and air rules thinking, ideas, social interaction, debate and questioning

Water – water is deep and healing and water rules feelings, intuition, quietness, relating, giving and sharing

MODES

There are three modes in astrology and four star signs allocated to each. The modes are:

cardinal – Aries, Cancer, Libra, Capricorn
fixed – Taurus, Leo, Scorpio, Aquarius
mutable – Gemini, Virgo, Sagittarius, Pisces

What each mode represents:

Cardinal – The first group represents the leaders of the zodiac, and these signs love to initiate and take action. Some say they're controlling.

Fixed – The middle group holds fast and stands the middle ground and acts as a stable, reliable companion. Some say they're stubborn.

Mutable – The last group is more willing to go with the flow and let life drift. They're more flexible and adaptable and often dual-natured. Some say they're all over the place.

INTROVERT AND EXTROVERT SIGNS/ OPPOSITE SIGNS

The introvert signs are the earth and water signs and the extrovert signs are the fire and air signs. Both sets oppose each other across the zodiac.

The 'introvert' earth and water oppositions are:

- Taurus – • Scorpio
- Cancer – • Capricorn
- Virgo – • Pisces

The 'extrovert' air and fire oppositions are:

- Aries – · Libra
- Gemini – · Sagittarius
- Leo – · Aquarius

THE HOUSES

The houses of the astrology wheel are an additional component to Sun sign horoscopes. The symmetry that is inherent within astrology remains, as the wheel is divided into twelve equal sections, called 'houses'. Each of the twelve houses is governed by one of the twelve zodiac signs.

There is an overlap in meaning as you move round the houses. Once you know the symbolism of all the star signs, it can be fleshed out further by learning about the areas of life represented by the twelve houses.

The houses provide more specific information if you choose to have a detailed birth chart reading.

This is based not only on your day of birth, which reveals your star sign, but also your time and place of birth. Here's the complete list of the meanings of the twelve houses and the zodiac sign they are ruled by:

1 – **Aries:** self, physical body, personal goals

2 – **Taurus:** money, possessions, values

3 – **Gemini:** communication, education, siblings, local neighbourhood

4 – **Cancer:** home, family, roots, the past, ancestry

5 – **Leo:** creativity, romance, entertainment, children, luck

6 – **Virgo:** work, routine, health, service

7 – **Libra:** relationships, the 'other', enemies, contracts

8 – **Scorpio:** joint finances, other people's resources, all things hidden and taboo

9 – **Sagittarius:** travel, study, philosophy, legal affairs, publishing, religion

10 – Capricorn: career, vocation, status, reputation

11 – **Aquarius:** friends, groups, networks, social responsibilities

12 – **Pisces:** retreat, sacrifice, spirituality

A GUIDE TO LOVE MATCHES

The star signs relate to each other in different ways depending on their essential nature. It can also be helpful to know the pattern they create across the zodiac. Here's a quick guide that relates to the chapter on Love Matches:

Two Peas In A Pod – the same star sign

Opposites Attract – star signs opposite each other

Soulmates – five or seven signs apart, and a traditional 'soulmate' connection

In Your Element – four signs apart, which means you share the same element

Squaring Up To Each Other – three signs apart, which means you share the same mode

Sexy Sextiles – two signs apart, which means you're both 'introverts' or 'extroverts'

Next Door Neighbours – one sign apart, different in nature but often share close connections